INSPIRATIONAL

Messages

for Daily

Encouragement

A 30-DAY RESOURCE TO UPLIFT YOU IN YOUR DAILY LIVING FOR GOD

CONNIE LYNNE ELLIOTT

Trilogy Christian Publishers
A Wholly Owned Subsidiary of Trinity Broadcasting Network
2442 Michelle Drive
Tustin, CA 92780

Author's photo and Cover photo by Neil Schillinger of 954Studios.com.

Cover design by: Cornerstone Creative Solutions

For information, address Trilogy Christian Publishing
Rights Department, 2442 Michelle Drive, Tustin, Ca 92780.
Trilogy Christian Publishing/ TBN and colophon are trademarks of Trinity Broadcasting Network.

For information about special discounts for bulk purchases, please contact Trilogy Christian Publishing.

Manufactured in the United States of America

10 9 8 7 6 5 4 3 2 1

Library of Congress Cataloging-in-Publication Data is available.

ISBN 978-1-63769-152-6 (Print Book)
ISBN 978-1-63769-153-3 (ebook)

DEDICATION

This book is dedicated to my husband, Leslie Elliott, who has been my lifelong best friend, encourager, protector, supporter, and companion. He is a loving nurturer who has watched me grow into the woman God created me to be. Leslie inspires me to continually seek God with my whole heart which allows me to grow and mature in my relationship with God. Through building my relationship with God, I am encouraged to walk out the destiny that God has placed before me. I am so blessed to have such a wonderful man of God at my side.

Leslie, God made you just for me and I am so honored to be your wife.

CONTENTS

ABOUT THE BOOK COVER

My husband and I wanted to go to Hawaii on our honeymoon in 1987, but we were not in a financial place to do so. As the years progressed and our family grew, going to Hawaii remained a dream. Every year on our anniversary, we would talk and dream about going to Hawaii. In 2017, I put together a vision board with goals and dreams. On the vision board were two pictures of Hawaii and I included Bible scriptures as we believed God for this dream to come to pass in our life. When the vision board was up and hanging on our wall, we planted a seed in the offering at church for this dream. God wonderfully worked it all out and in May of 2019, we boarded the plane with my brother and his wife and headed to Hawaii for two weeks; one week on a seven-day cruise around the Hawaiian Islands and one week on land. It was a beautiful trip! I thank God for His goodness in bringing this dream to pass in our lives and we were able to pay for the whole trip in cash.

The cover photo was taken in Hawaii on the last day of our cruise around the islands as we traveled up the Na Pali Coast. What a true inspiration of God's beauty. My brother and his wife took this amazing picture that has been chosen as the book cover.

I want to share with you the scriptures my husband and I stood on while trusting God to bring this dream to pass in our lives:

"I make known the end from the beginning, from ancient times, what is still to come. I say, 'My purpose will stand, and I will do all that I please'" (Isa. 46:10 NIV).

Then the Lord replied: "Write down the revelation and make it plain on tablets so that a herald may run with it. For the revelation awaits an appointed time; it speaks of the end and will not prove false. Though it linger, wait for it; it will certainly come and will not delay."
Habakkuk 2:2–3 (NIV)

"You have given him his heart's desire and have not withheld the request of his lips. Selah" (Ps. 21:2 ESV).

"Take delight in the Lord, and He will give you your heart's desires. Commit everything you do to the Lord. Trust Him, and He will help you" (Ps. 37: 4–5 (NLT).

"Seek the kingdom of God above all else, and live righteously, and He will give you everything you need" (Matt. 6:33 NLT).

Ask and it will be given to you; seek and you will find; knock and the door will be opened to you. For everyone who asks receives; the one who seeks finds; and to the one who knocks, the door will be opened.

Matthew 7:7–8 (NIV)

ACKNOWLEDGMENTS

Many people have inspired and impacted my journey in life. When I look back, I am so thankful for the goodness of God and how He sent people into my life to help me, encourage me, inspire me, and give me hope for a brighter future. I would like to acknowledge and recognize the following groups of people:

- To God, my heavenly Father, through the guidance of the Holy Spirit, made this book possible.
- To my mother, Lorraine Forsling, who inspired me with stories of nursing as a young girl that impacted my life to become a registered nurse.
- To my sister, Dorene Titus, who spent time with me as a child, talking to me about Jesus and encouraging me to pray to God even before I understood there was a God.
- To my dear friend, Joyce Ohl. She graciously allowed me to be a part of her family in my teen years that showed me hope, inspiration, and encouragement in marriage and family.
- To my dad and stepmom, Dean and LaVon Titus, who continuously prayed and encouraged me to keep my faith, trust, and dependency in the Word of God.
- To my pastors, throughout my life who continually fed me the Word of God to advance growth and maturity in my walk with God.

- To my brother Neil Schillinger, of Neil Schillinger Photography, and his wife, Ann-Marie Serrano, who captured the most inspiring picture for my book cover while we vacationed and explored Hawaii together.

PREFACE

A few years ago when I was a nurse and educator in women and children services, I had the opportunity to train multiple nurses on how to become a labor and delivery nurse. At the beginning of the nursing orientation, I would always ask them one very important question: "How do you learn best?" Their answers would help guide me through the training process and optimize the nurses' learning opportunities.

A teacher/educator must understand where the student is in the learning process to continually move them forward in new skills, experience, and develop their knowledge. The ultimate goal of orientation is for the nurse to function independently, which can vary in time depending on their skill level, attitude, and involvement in orientation.

To have a successful orientation, the teacher/educator should be approachable, kind, dedicated, calm, flexible, and preferably, possess a sense of humor. Those quality traits will provide a positive cultural learning environment for the nurse to grow in skill and knowledge, and this will set the environment for the nurse to enjoy coming to work.

How many times have you tried to learn something new and you came across someone with a negative attitude or was told it could only be done one way which was really "only their way?" When that occurs, it squelches credibility with the teacher/educator and now the nurse feels like they are walking on eggshells while trying to successfully complete their orientation.

God has given each of us gifts and talents. We are all unique and when we come together as a team, we can help each other perform optimally to achieve goals. When a person wants to go to the top of a mountain, you realize there are many ways to get to the top. You can hike, take a train, bike, run, walk, take a bus, drive a car, or even jump out of an airplane to glide over the top of the mountain. How you get there is up to you.

This book has been written as a vehicle for you to be inspired as you walk with God in your journey of life. Just as climbing the mountain, some days walking with the Lord can be more challenging than others but, on the days where you may feel you're in the valley, press into the Word of God. Don't give up on the promises that God has given to you.

The point is, we all learn differently. This book is packed with different ways of learning utilizing visual and written scripture that are captured through pictures, thirty daily inspiring messages, testimonies, and biblical stories, all to optimize your learning in order to increase your faith in the Word of God so you can live out the desires and dreams that God has placed in your heart.

INTRODUCTION

As I was spending time in prayer and seeking God back in May 2020, He gave me the title of this book and said this would be the next book for me to write. *Inspirational Messages For Daily Encouragement: A 30-Day Resource to Uplift You in Your Daily Living* will inspire and encourage you to walk out your faith in God with assurance, boldness, and confidence. You will have the opportunity to visually see the beauty of God's creation with the written Word of God and be guided through short, captivating, and inspirational messages to help you grow and mature in your walk with God. Additionally, you will read personal testimonies from people who held onto the Word of God until they achieved victory in their life. You will also read stories from the Bible to strengthen your faith and give you hope.

As you read through this book, let each picture and the Word of God speak to your heart, and change your life. I found a quote that reminded me as I was creating this book: "One picture is worth a thousand words"— Fred Barnard. Each one of us will see something different when we look into the beauty of God's creation through word and picture. Let God speak to your heart each day as you meditate on His Word.

Section 1

---

30 Days of Inspirational Messages to Uplift You in Your Daily Living

DAY 1 FAITH

"If you have faith as small as
a mustard seed, you can say
to this mountain, 'Move from
here to there,' and it will move.
Nothing will be impossible for
you" (Matt. 17:20 NIV).

"And without faith it is impossible
to please God, because anyone who
comes to Him must believe that He
exists and that He rewards those who
earnestly seek Him" (Heb.11:6 NIV).

What does your life look like today? What if you closed your eyes and imagined what your life could look like six months to one year from now if you just made a few changes? No matter what your situation may look like today, it can change. Seek God and ask for His help to make the necessary changes. Matthew 19:26 (ESV) says, "...with man this is impossible, but with God all things are possible." God is the God of possibility. We must have faith. Hebrews 11:1 (NIV) says, "Now faith is confidence in what we hope for and assurance about what we do not see." I encourage you to put your trust in God and declare new things for your future as it is written in Isaiah 46:10 (NLT). It says, "Only I can tell you the future before it even happens. Everything I plan will come to pass, for I do whatever I wish." Have a glorious day.

DAY 2 HEALING

"Then they cried to the Lord in their trouble, and He saved them from their distress. He sent out His word and healed them; He rescued them from the grave. Let them give thanks to the Lord for His unfailing love and His wonderful deeds for mankind" (Ps. 107:19–21 NIV).

Do you need God to heal something in your body? I want to encourage you to read the Word of God and meditate on the scriptures. Matthew, Mark, Luke, and John are full of accounts where Jesus went around praying for the sick and healed them. Jesus died for us so that we could be healed and walk in divine health. Luke 4:38–40 (NLT) says:

> After leaving the synagogue that day,
> Jesus went to Simon's home, where
> He found Simon's mother-in-law
> very sick with a high fever. "Please
> heal her," everyone begged. Standing
> at her bedside, He rebuked the fever,
> and it left her. And she got up at once
> and prepared a meal for them. As the
> sun went down that evening, people
> throughout the village brought sick
> family members to Jesus. No matter
> what their diseases were, the touch
> of His hand healed every one.

Glory to God! As a child of God, we are entitled to health and healing in our bodies. In 3 John 1:2 (NLT) it says, "Dear friend, I hope all is well with you and that you are as healthy in body as you are strong in spirit." As you meditate on this story and the scriptures, keep them close to your heart. Have a glorious day.

DAY 3 HOPE

"The Lord on high *is* mightier
Than the noise of many waters,
Than the mighty waves of
the sea" (Ps. 93:4 NKJV).

Have you ever had a week where you were so excited about what God was doing in your life and then out of nowhere, you get slammed with challenges and obstacles? Psalm 93:4 (NKJV) says, "The Lord on high is mightier than the noise of many waters, than the mighty waves of the sea." This scripture reminds us that no matter what *noise* comes our way, whether it be the loss of a loved one, a financial upset, discouraging news, or setbacks, God is mightier than all of it. He is still God and He will make a way for you. Isaiah 43:16 (NLT) says, "I am the Lord, who opened a way through the waters, making a dry path through the sea." Whatever your circumstance may be, remember it is temporary! Speak to the storm in your life and tell it to be still. Psalms 107:29 (NLT) says, "He calmed the storm to a whisper and stilled the waves." I pray that you will meditate on these scriptures and keep them close to your heart today. Have a wonderful day.

DAY 4 JOY

"Rejoice always, pray continually, give thanks in all circumstances; for this is God's will for you in Christ Jesus" (1 Thess. 5:16–18 NIV).

What a magnificent day to wake up and see the beauty of God's creation. Have you ever woken up early in the morning, poured yourself a cup of tea or coffee, and sat outside to admire the beauty of the morning sunrise? All the different colors in the sky, the light that over-shadows the fields, or the clouds that hover over the ponds and lakes are breathtaking. As you breathe in the fresh morning air and hear the birds arise to praise their Creator, you exalt your praises to God for His excellence in detail and spectacular beauty. You begin to rejoice in the goodness of God knowing that He is the one who gives us joy and strength. Exodus 15:2 (ESV) says, "The Lord is my strength and my song, and He has become my salvation. He is my God, and I will praise Him, my father's God, and I will exalt Him." Isaiah 12:2 (NLT) says, "See, God has come to save me. I will trust in Him and not be afraid. The Lord God is my strength and my song; He has given me victory." Therefore, no matter what circumstances may come our way, we can keep our eyes fixed on God and His promises, rejoice in His goodness and trust Him to see us through. I encourage you to meditate on these scriptures and keep them close to your heart today. Have a blessed and joyful day.

DAY 5 PEACE

"Peace I leave with you; My peace I give you. I do not give to you as the world gives. Do not let your hearts be troubled and do not be afraid" (John 14:27 NIV).

"The Lord lift up His countenance upon you, And give you peace" (Num. 6:26 NKJV).

Day 5 Peace Devotional

Have you ever thought to yourself, "I don't know how much more I can bear?" We all know life happens and sometimes it can be so overwhelming. If you're in this situation, you might be saying to yourself, *I could use some peace in my life.* Well, there is good news for you. John 14:1 (NIV) says, "Do not let your hearts be troubled. You believe in God; believe also in me." When you look to God and seek Him, ask to be filled with His peace. Philippians 4:7 (NLT) says, "Then you will experience God's peace, which exceeds anything we can understand. His peace will guard your hearts and minds as you live in Christ Jesus." I encourage you to meditate on these scriptures and keep them close to your heart today. Have a wonderful and peaceful day.

DAY 6 PROSPERITY

"The Lord was with Joseph so that he prospered…" (Gen. 39:21 NIV).

"Surely, Lord, you bless the righteous; you surround them with your favor as with a shield" (Ps. 5:12 NIV).

Did you know that God desires His children to be prosperous? 3 John 1:2 (NKJV) says, "Beloved, I pray that you may prosper in all things and be in health, just as your soul prospers. It also says in Deuteronomy 8:18 (NIV), "But remember the Lord your God, for it is He who gives you the ability to produce wealth, and so confirms His covenant, which He swore to your ancestors, as it is today." If you are struggling with your finances and are doubting your beliefs about God wanting you to live an abundant life, then I encourage you to meditate on these scriptures and stir up your faith in the Word of God. 2 Corinthians 9:8 (NLT) says, "And God will generously provide all you need. Then you will always have everything you need and plenty left over to share with others." Not only does God want you abundantly blessed, but He also wants you in a position where you can bless other people from the overflow of God's blessings in your life. I pray this word encourages you today. Have a blessed, favored, and prosperous day.

DAY 7 WISDOM

"And He said to them, "Go into all the world and preach the gospel to every creature" (Mark 16:15 NKJV).

"Come, follow me," Jesus said, "and I will send you out to fish for people" (Matt. 4:19 NIV).

When I look at this picture, it reminds me of the "Great Commission." The rowboat is empty! We want to leave *no one* behind but rather fish for Jesus so everyone can spend eternity in heaven. Matthew 28:16–20 (ESV) says, "Now the eleven disciples went to Galilee, to the mountain to which Jesus had directed them. And when they saw Him they worshiped Him, but some doubted. And Jesus came and said to them, 'All authority in heaven and on earth has been given to me. Go therefore and make disciples of all nations, baptizing them in the name of the Father and of the Son and of the Holy Spirit, teaching them to observe all that I have commanded you. And behold, I am with you always, to the end of the age.'" Mark 16:15 (ESV) says, "And He said to them, 'Go into all the world and proclaim the gospel to the whole creation.'" I pray this word encourages you today and you keep these scriptures close to your heart. Have a wonderful day.

DAY 8 FAITH, THANKFULNESS, AND TRUST

"I am yours…"
(Psalms 119:94 ESV).

"In Him and through faith in Him
we may approach God with freedom
and confidence" (Eph. 3:12 NIV).

Day 8 Faith, Thankfulness, and Trust Devotional

Are you in a place of uncertainty in your life? Do you know in your heart there is something more for you but just don't know what it is or how to achieve it? Psalm 119:105 (NLT) says, "Your word is a lamp to guide my feet and a light for my path." God will order your steps. Psalms 37:23 (NLT) says, "The Lord directs the steps of the godly. He delights in every detail of their lives." Isaiah 52:12 (GNT) says, "This time you will not have to leave in a hurry; you will not be trying to escape. The Lord your God will lead you and protect you on every side." I encourage you to seek God and remain steadfast in the Word of God. Keep these scriptures close to your heart and remain confident in God knowing that He is on your side and guiding your every step. Have a glorious day.

DAY 9 ENCOURAGEMENT

NEWS FLASH

"Worry weighs a person down; an encouraging word cheers a person up" (Prov. 12:25 NLT).

"Give your burdens to the Lord, and He will take care of you. He will not permit the godly to slip and fall" (Ps. 55:22 NLT).

"Give all your worries and cares to God, for He cares about you" (1 Peter 5:7 NLT).

Are you feeling overwhelmed with the affairs of life? The pressure can bombard us as we face challenges, obstacles, and disappointment. Today, I want to encourage you with the scripture in John 14:27 (NLT). It says, "I am leaving you with a gift—peace of mind and heart. And the peace I give is a gift the world cannot give. So don't be troubled or afraid." 2 Thessalonians 3:16 (NLT) says, "Now may the Lord of peace Himself give you His peace at all times and in every situation. The Lord be with you all." Sometimes we just need to remind ourselves that God wants us to live out our lives with the peace of God. As you ponder on these scriptures, know that God covers you in His perfect peace as you handle the affairs of life. Have a great day.

DAY 10 FAITH

"You are faithful"
(Heb. 10:23 NKJV).

Did you know that Deuteronomy 7:9 (NIV) says, "Know therefore that the LORD your God is God; He is the faithful God, keeping His covenant of love to a thousand generations of those who love Him and keep His commandments." We have an assurance that God's Word says He is faithful! Lamentations 3:22–23 (ESV) says, "The steadfast love of the Lord never ceases; His mercies never come to an end; they are new every morning; great is your faithfulness. As you meditate on these scriptures, be confident that God cares about every detail of your life. I encourage you to reflect on everything God has done for you and praise Him for His faithfulness in all things. Have a wonderful day.

DAY 11 HEALING

"He heals the brokenhearted and binds up their wounds. He determines the number of the stars; He gives to all of them their names. Great is our Lord, and abundant in power; His understanding is beyond measure" (Ps. 147:3–5 ESV).

Day 11 Healing Devotional

We have all experienced loss, whether it was an unborn baby, a child, a spouse, mother, father, friend, or other loved ones. This can be a very difficult time in our lives, and some may even ask, what and why? The pain of loss can be so great that it is unbearable just to get out of bed in the morning. I encourage you to lift your arms and eyes unto the Lord, for your help will come from Him. He knows exactly how to help you go through the grieving process and come out stronger on the other side. Psalms 34:18 (NLT) says, "The Lord is close to the brokenhearted; He rescues those whose spirits are crushed.

As you go throughout your day, keep this scripture close to your heart, "Even when I walk through a valley of deep darkness, I will not be afraid because you are with me. Your rod and Your staff—they comfort me." Psalms 23:4 (ISV). This scripture reveals to us that we will walk through it. I encourage you to seek God and allow Him to heal your heart. Have an amazing day.

DAY 12 HOPE

"Though he falls, he will
not be overwhelmed, for the
Lord is holding his hand" (Ps.
37:24 Berean Study Bible).

"Lord, sustain me as you promised,
that I may live! Do not let my hope
be crushed" (Ps. 119:116 NLT).

Have you ever said, "*Enough is enough?*" You cry out to God asking for help to get you through life's challenges, disappointments, and uncertainties. We have all experienced those moments from time to time. Psalm 39:7 (ISV) says, "How long, Lord, will I wait expectantly? I have placed my hope in you."

If you are experiencing this "I am fed up" feeling in your life, I want to encourage you to keep hoping, keep believing, and keep trusting in God. Isaiah 43:2 (ESV) says, "When you pass through the waters, I will be with you; and through the rivers, they shall not overwhelm you; when you walk through fire you shall not be burned, and the flame shall not consume you." God can deliver you! I pray that God gives you wisdom, insight, and direction in how to handle your life circumstances as you seek God and meditate on His word. Have an insightful day.

DAY 13 JOY

"But may all who seek you rejoice and be glad in you; may those who long for your saving help always say, 'The Lord is great!'" (Ps. 70:4 NIV).

"...rejoice with joy unspeakable..." (1 Peter 1:8 KJV).

As you go throughout your day, I pray that you are filled with the joy of the Lord. Let your joy and happiness be shared with others. You never know what a smile or laugh will do for someone. Proverbs 17:22 (NLT) says, "A cheerful heart is good medicine, but a broken spirit saps a person's strength."

I was told a long time ago by my lovely stepmother, "As a nurse, never take hope away from people." People have to be able to hang onto hope to keep purpose in their life. Psalm 27:7–8 (ESV) says, "The Lord is my strength and my shield; in Him my heart trusts, and I am helped; my heart exults, and with my song I give thanks to Him. The Lord is the strength of His people; He is the saving refuge of His anointed." I pray this word encourages you today to spread some joy and help increase someone's strength. Have a delightful day.

DAY 14 PEACE

"Come to me, all you who are weary and burdened, and I will give you rest" (Matt. 11:28 NIV).

Sometimes in life, we are so busy burning the candle at both ends that we don't stop to rest. We must allow ourselves to rest. Jesus told His disciples in Mark 6:31 (NLT), "Let's go off by ourselves to a quiet place and rest awhile." Even God rested. Genesis 2:2 (NLT) says, "On the seventh day God had finished His work of creation, so He rested from all His work." When we rest, it allows our mind, body, and soul to be renewed; and our body to be strengthened. The next time you are running around trying to accomplish everything, take a deep breath, sit down, relax, and prioritize what needs to be done and what could wait until the next day. As you hold these scriptures close to your heart today, let them guide you with wisdom on how to manage your time more efficiently. In doing this, it will provide you with much-needed rest. Have a calm and relaxing day.

DAY 15 PROSPERITY

"He is like a tree planted by
streams of water that yields its
fruit in its season, and its leaf does
not wither. In all that he does,
he prospers" (Ps. 1:3 ESV).

Did you know that God wants you to prosper in everything that you put your hands to? I love the verse, Deuteronomy 28:8 (NIV). It says, "The Lord will send a blessing on your barns and on everything you put your hand to. The Lord your God will bless you in the land He is giving you." It also says in Deuteronomy 15:10 (NIV) to, "Give generously to them and do so without a grudging heart; then because of this the Lord your God will bless you in all your work and in everything you put your hand to." Now that is something to shout about! God does not want you to have a lack in any area of your life. When Jesus died on the cross for our sins, He took away poverty so we could live an abundant life. John 10:10 (NLT) says, "The thief's purpose is to steal and kill and destroy. My purpose is to give them a rich and satisfying life." As you meditate on these scriptures, I pray you are encouraged and have a greater understanding of what belongs to you as a child of God. Have a glorious day.

DAY 16 WISDOM

"The fear of the Lord is the beginning of knowledge, but fools despise wisdom and instruction" (Prov. 1:7 NIV).

"If any of you lacks wisdom, you should ask God, who gives generously to all without finding fault, and it will be given to you" (James 1:5 NIV).

Have you ever been in a situation where you didn't know what to do? The Bible says in James 1:5 (NIV), "If any of you lacks wisdom, you should ask God, who gives generously to all without finding fault, and it will be given to you." This verse brings reassurance to our life of how important we are to our Heavenly Father. God cares about our everyday life choices and situations we are involved in. Matthew 7:7 (NIV) says, "Ask and it will be given to you; seek and you will find; knock and the door will be opened to you." As you go throughout your day, I encourage you to ask God for help, no matter how big or small the request. He has given the Holy Spirit to lead us, guide us, and provide insight into everything we do. Have a tremendous day!

DAY 17 FAITH, THANKFULNESS, AND TRUST

"For the Spirit God gave us does not make us timid, but gives us power, love and self-discipline" (2 Timothy 1:7 NIV).

Day 17 Faith, Thankfulness, and Trust Devotional

Did you know that we do not have to live with fear in our life? 2 Timothy 1:7 (NLT) says, "For God has not given us a spirit of fear and timidity, but of power, love, and self-discipline." Isaiah 41:10 (NLT) says, "Don't be afraid, for I am with you. Don't be discouraged, for I am your God. I will strengthen you and help you. I will hold you up with my victorious right hand." These scriptures reminded me of Deuteronomy 31:6 (NLT). It says, "So be strong and courageous! Do not be afraid and do not panic before them. For the LORD your God will personally go ahead of you. He will neither fail you nor abandon you." So, keep your eyes on the Lord and trust in Him. I pray you hold these scriptures close to your heart and remember, "There is no fear in love. But perfect love drives out fear…" 1 John 4:18 (NIV). Have a loving and peaceful day.

DAY 18 ENCOURAGEMENT

"But I tell you, love your enemies and pray for those who persecute you, that you may be children of your Father in heaven…" (Matt. 5:44–45 NIV).

"But I say to you who hear, love your enemies, do good to those who hate you, bless those who curse you, pray for those who mistreat you" (Luke 6:27–28 NASB).

Who doesn't love a long-stemmed rose? They come in different colors and different smells. My favorite rose is the red Chrysler Imperial. It is a beautiful flower with a strong fragrance. Although the flower displays its beauty, you can get hurt by the thorns on the stem when you cut them.

So let me ask you a question. How many times have you been around someone who just rubbed you the wrong way? It doesn't matter what they do—it just irritates you! When that happens, I want you to think about the long-stemmed rose. People may have the outward beauty, but deep down they are hurt and insecure. We have no idea what is going on in another person's life for them to respond the way they do. We need to stay in love and pray for them. As we pray, God can work in their lives to help them. Luke 6:38 (NIV) says, "Give, and it will be given to you. A good measure, pressed down, shaken together and running over, will be poured into your lap. For with the measure you use, it will be measured to you." If you want love, sow love. If you want kindness, sow kindness. If you want forgiveness, then forgive. Remember today to sow seeds of love, kindness, and forgiveness. I pray that the beauty of your life will help people all around you. Have an exquisite day!

DAY 19 FAITH

"I will sing of the steadfast love of
the LORD, forever; with my mouth
I will make known your faithfulness
to all generations" (Ps. 89:1 ESV).

"To you, O Lord, I lift up
my soul" (Ps. 25:1 ESV).

Have you ever been so full of the Word of God that your heart is overjoyed in your faith in God? I pray you are continually encouraged and strengthened in your walk with the Lord. I love the verse in Psalm 27:4 (ERV). It says, "One thing have I asked of the Lord, that will I seek after; that I may dwell in the house of the Lord all the days of my life, to behold the beauty of the Lord, and to inquire in His temple."

Maybe this isn't you at all. Maybe you are going through a rough time in your life and doing everything you can just to get through the day. If that is you, maybe you just need a power recharge in your life. I encourage you to ask God for help. He will fill you with His love, kindness, peace, and restore your hope.

When the battery on your phone loses power, you plug it in. When you feel empty and don't have anything more to give, that is when your internal battery light flashes, "Alert! Caution!" or you may just break down and cry. If that is your situation, there is hope. Set aside some time, even if it's only five minutes, to pray and worship God. You will be amazed at how quickly your faith is recharged and your heart is filled with peace and joy. Have a blissful day.

DAY 20 HEALING

GOD IS MY HEALER

"My child, pay attention to what I say. Listen carefully to my words. Don't lose sight of them. Let them penetrate deep into your heart, for they bring life to those who find them, and healing to their whole body" (Prov. 4: 20–22 NLT).

What comes to your mind when you think of healing? Most people would think about physical healing but God wants your entire being healed; spiritually, physically, mentally, and emotionally. Psalm 107:20 (ESV) says, "He sent out His word and healed them." That means God wants you healed and delivered emotionally, physically, and mentally. 3 John 1:2 (KJV) says, "Beloved, I pray that you may prosper in all things and be in health, just as your soul prospers."

So, what kind of healing do you need today? This is tough because it requires us to look deep in our hearts to analyze our life and behavior. You may be experiencing emotional or anger outbursts in your life and are not for sure where it is coming from. I assure you it stems from past hurts that have been tucked away and have never been addressed. I encourage you to get alone with God and pray this prayer.

Dear Heavenly Father,

Your word says in Colossians 3:12–13 (NIV), "Therefore, as God's chosen people, holy and dearly loved, clothe yourselves with compassion, kindness, humility, gentleness, and patience. Bear with each other and forgive one another if any of you has a grievance against someone. Forgive as the Lord forgave you." So, God, I come before you asking for insight and truth in my life. I have been hurt and need help with forgiveness. Please forgive me for holding onto this hurtful situation and I choose to forgive [say the name(s)] and release them to you right now. Fill my life with your healing power of love that I can live freely before you. In Jesus' name.

DAY 21 HOPE

"Let your hope make you glad. Be patient in time of trouble and never stop praying" (Rom. 12:12 CEV).

"And the Scriptures were written to teach and encourage us by giving us hope" (Rom. 15:4 CEV).

We can arise in the morning with anticipation knowing God is good. Are you hoping for something to come to pass in your life, marriage, children, family, job, or finances? Let the Word of God fill you with hope as you read and meditate on the scriptures. My prayer for you today is found in Ephesians 1:18 (NLT). "I pray that your hearts will be flooded with light so that you can understand the confident hope He has given to those He called—His holy people who are His rich and glorious inheritance." Have a fabulous day!

DAY 22 JOY

"I will sing of the steadfast love of the Lord, forever; with my mouth I will make known your faithfulness to all generations" (Ps. 89:1 ESV).

"I will tell them, 'God's love can always be trusted, and His faithfulness lasts as long as the heavens'" (Ps. 89:2 CEV).

Greetings on this lovely day. Did you know that you can wake up with a song in your heart to the Lord? Psalms 98:1 (ESV) says, "Oh sing to the Lord a new song, for He has done marvelous things!" No matter what circumstances or challenges come your way, we have a God who loves us. I want to encourage you to keep your chin up and stand firm in your faith. Thank God for His goodness and trust Him that He will bring you through. Circumstances come and go, but the Word of God stays true for eternity. Psalms 104:33 (NIV) says, "I will sing to the Lord all my life; I will sing praise to my God as long as I live." As you go throughout your day, I pray your heart is filled with songs of praise. Have a joyful day.

DAY 23 PEACE

"Peace be with you!"
(John 20:21 NIV).

"So then, let us follow after things
which make for peace, and things
by which we may build one another
up" (Rom. 14:19 NHEB).

Good morning! As you go throughout your day, I pray the Lord gives you strength and blesses you with peace. Colossians 3:15 (GNT) says, "The peace that Christ gives is to guide you in the decisions you make; for it is to this peace that God has called you together in the one body. And be thankful." Be encouraged today that whatever crosses your path, you can remain in peace as you keep your eyes fixed on God. Meditate on the words of John 14:27 (NIV), "Peace I leave with you; my peace I give you. I do not give to you as the world gives. Do not let your hearts be troubled and do not be afraid." Have a splendid day.

DAY 24 PROSPERITY

"Seek the kingdom of God above all else, and live righteously, and He will give you everything you need" (Matt. 6:33 NLT).

"With me are riches and honor, enduring wealth and prosperity" (Prov. 8:18 NIV).

In everything you do, seek God for His direction. He desires for His children to have a joyful, healthy, and prosperous life. Luke 12:31(NLT) says, "But seek His kingdom, and these things will be added unto you." God doesn't want you to worry about what you will eat, drink, or be clothed in. He desires for you to have every need met in your life without worry and be a blessing to those around you.

As a child of God, our covenant includes Deuteronomy 28:2 (NIV) that says, "All these blessings will come on you and accompany you if you obey the Lord your God." So, if we obey the voice of the Lord our God, then our lives should reflect the following blessings as described in Deuteronomy 28:3–13. NIV unless other translation is specified.

- You will be blessed in the city and blessed in the country.
- The fruit of your womb will be blessed, and the crops of your land and the young of your livestock—the calves of your herds and the lambs of your flocks.
- Your basket and your kneading trough will be blessed.
- You will be blessed when you come in and blessed when you go out.

- The Lord will grant that the enemies who rise up against you will be defeated before you. They will come at you from one direction but flee from you in seven.
- The Lord will send a blessing on your barns and on everything you put your hand to. The Lord your God will bless you in the land He is giving you.
- The Lord will establish you as a people holy to Himself, as He has sworn to you, if you keep the commandments of the Lord your God and walk in His ways. (ESV)
- Then all the nations of the world will see that you are a people claimed by the Lord, and they will stand in awe of you. (NLT)
- The Lord will grant you abundant prosperity—in the fruit of your womb, the young of your livestock and the crops of your ground—in the land He swore to your ancestors to give you.
- The Lord will open the heavens, the storehouse of His bounty, to send rain on your land in season and to bless all the work of your hands. You will lend to many nations but will borrow from none.
- The Lord will make you the head, not the tail. If you pay attention to the commands of the Lord your God that I give you this day and carefully follow them, you will always be at the top, never at the bottom.

We are then instructed in Deuteronomy 28:14 (NIV), "Do not turn aside from any of the commands I give you today, to the right or to the left, following other gods and serving them."

We see in scripture that as we have a relationship with God and seek after Him that He will take care of every need and abundantly bless us. He gave us His covenant and His Word as our authentication. I pray you are encouraged today as you meditate on the blessings of God for your life. Have a prosperous day.

DAY 25 WISDOM

"And look at ships! They are so big that it takes strong winds to drive them, yet they are steered by a tiny rudder wherever the helmsman directs" (James 3:4 ISV).

"A word out of your mouth may seem of no account, but it can accomplish nearly anything—or destroy it!" (James 3:5 MSG).

Do you remember the saying when we were kids, "Sticks and stones may break my bones, but words will never hurt me?" The truth is that words can hurt you and words can also create a beautiful future. Proverbs 18:21 (NIV) says, "Death and life are in the power of the tongue…" Speak what you want your life to look like, not what you see with your physical eye today. Change your future to line up with your dreams and goals. What do you want to achieve and where do you want to be six months, twelve months, three years, or five years from now? Isaiah 46:10 (NASB) says to declare the end from the beginning. I encourage you to follow the wisdom in Isaiah 46:10. Declare it, speak it, and watch your life change. Have a wonderful day.

DAY 26 FAITH, THANKFULNESS, AND TRUST

"For I know the plans I have for you," declares the LORD, "plans to prosper you and not to harm you, plans to give you hope and a future" (Jer, 29:11 NIV),

Day 26 Faith, Thankfulness, and Trust Devotional

Sometimes we can get so wrapped up in the details and perfections of life that it can lead us down a frustrating and displeasing path. God tells us not to worry or be anxious about anything. Philippians 4:6–7 (NLT) says, "Don't worry about anything; instead, pray about everything. Tell God what you need, and thank Him for all He has done. Then you will experience God's peace, which exceeds anything we can understand. His peace will guard your hearts and minds as you live in Christ Jesus." In other words, God's got this. You are probably thinking, *easier said than done*. We need to hold fast, trust, and believe that if God said it in His word, then so be it.

As you go throughout your day, reflect on Isaiah 26:3 (ESV). It says, "You keep him in perfect peace whose mind is stayed on You, because he trusts in You." How encouraging to know that we can live a life of peace as we keep our focus on God. So, as you seek God for His plan for your life, know that His plan will prosper you and give you hope and a future. Have a glorious day.

DAY 27 ENCOURAGEMENT

True encouragement comes from knowing the Encourager!

"I pray that God, the source of hope, will fill you completely with joy and peace because you trust in Him. Then you will overflow with confident hope through the power of the Holy Spirit" (Rom.15:13 NLT).

"And I will ask the Father, and He will give you another advocate to help you and be with you forever" (John 14:16 NLT).

We can all use some encouragement in our daily living, whether it is needed in our relationships, raising a family, schooling, or career. Encouragement helps us to keep focused and stay on track to pursue our goals and dreams. The good news is that we don't have to do this on our own. John 14:26 (CEV) says, "But the Holy Spirit will come and help you, because the Father will send the Spirit to take my place. The Spirit will teach you everything and will remind you of what I said while I was with you."

How encouraging to know that we are never in a situation by ourselves. Let's look at an example in life. If you were completing a math assignment and didn't understand how to do a math problem, you would ask your teacher. God knew we were going to need help so He sent the Holy Spirit to be our helper. The Holy Spirit can teach you and instruct you in how to accomplish the daily tasks and milestones in life. When we ask the Holy Spirit for His help, He will help us. Isaiah 11:2 (CEV) says, "The Spirit of the Lord will be with him to give him understanding, wisdom, and insight. He will be powerful, and he will know and honor the Lord." I pray the Encourager encourages you today. Have a great day!

DAY 28 FAITH

"No temptation has overtaken you that is not common to man. God is faithful, and He will not let you be tempted beyond your ability, but with the temptation He will also provide the way of escape, that you may be able to endure it" (1 Cor. 10:13 ESV).

In your course of life, remember to look to God and rely on the Holy Spirit for direction to the finish line. I have two sons who like to kayak. With each stroke of the paddle, they are moved closer and closer to their desired destination. On a river, some signs say "Throw trash here" or "Turn left instead of right." Just as you have signs to guide you along the river while kayaking, you have the Holy Spirit who will guide you throughout the course of life. He will detour you from falls and mishaps. Isaiah 43:16 (ESV) says, "Thus says the Lord, who makes a way in the sea, a path in the mighty waters." I encourage you to stay on track and keep focused on your dreams and goals. If you have fallen off the pathway, get back up and refocus. Keep your faith and trust in God knowing that He is the one showing you the way. Have a great day.

DAY 29 HEALING

"I am the Lord, and I do not change…" (Mal. 3:6 NLT).

"He strengthens those who are weak and tired" (Isa. 40:29 GNT).

Is it all you could do to get out of bed today? Do you need some energy and strength in your life? John 14:14 (ESV) says, "If you ask anything in my name, I will do it." Psalm 29:11 (NIV) says, "The Lord gives strength to His people; the Lord blesses His people with peace." Both these scriptures tell us that God wants us to live a blessed life full of strength and peace. I encourage you to meditate on the following scriptures and declare them over your life. Isaiah 40:29–31 (NIV) says,

> He gives strength to the weary and
> increases the power of the weak.
> Even youths grow tired and weary,
> and young men stumble and fall;
> but those who hope in the Lord
> will renew their strength. They
> will soar on wings like eagles;
> they will run and not grow weary,
> they will walk and not be faint.

I pray you have a restful day full of strength and peace as you meditate on the Word of God.

DAY 30 HOPE

"Friends, when life gets really difficult, don't jump to the conclusion that God isn't on the job. Instead, be glad that you are in the very thick of what Christ experienced. This is a spiritual refining process, with glory just around the corner" (1 Peter 4:12–13 MSG).

Did you know that God is working out all things for your benefit? I encourage you to keep your eyes fixed on God and He will show you the direction for your life. As you go throughout your day, keep this scripture close to your heart, "And we know that God causes all things to work together for good to those who love God, to those who are called according to His purpose" (Rom. 8:28 NASB). This scripture reveals to us that no matter what is going on in our life, God is working for us, to help us, in our situation and circumstance. Thank God that He is helping you through the temporary conditions in life.

During these periods in our life is when we need to have patience and trust God. Ephesians 1:11–12 (NIV) says,

> In Him we were also chosen, having been predestined according to the plan of Him who works out everything in conformity with the purpose of His will, in order that we, who were the first to put our hope in Christ, might be for the praise of His glory.

As we close out Section 1, I pray that the pictures, Bible scriptures, and short, inspiring messages helped you grow and mature in your walk with God. The next section of this book will be a continuation of encouragement as you read personal testimonies from people who held onto the Word of God until they achieved victory in their life. Additionally, you will read stories from the Bible that will strengthen your faith and give you hope while you are trusting God for your dreams, desires, and goals to manifest in your life. Have an amazing day.

Section 2

REAL PEOPLE, REAL STORIES, REAL TESTIMONIES

Have you ever asked yourself what is a testimony and why do we testify? A testimony is simply sharing stories of how God brought you through situations and circumstances in your life. We testify to give God praise and thanksgiving for what He has done in our lives. When we testify, it strengthens our faith and encourages us and others to keep their faith and trust in God. 1 Thessalonians 5:11 (NIV) says, "Therefore encourage one another and build each other up, just as in fact you are doing." If God didn't think encouragement was necessary, He wouldn't have told us in His Word or sent us the Holy Spirit to encourage us.

Let me ask, what has God done for you? Maybe He helped you get out of bed today with no pain in your legs or hips. Maybe He gave you strength and courage to get up and walk after an injury. Maybe, He helped you see your grandchildren who you haven't seen in a while. Maybe He helped you work through an emotional upset in your life. Whatever God has done for you, thank Him. God cares about every detail of your life. Matthew 6:33 (NLT) says, "Seek the kingdom of God above all else, and live righteously, and He will give you everything you need." Psalms 37:4 (ESV) says, "Delight yourself in the Lord, and He will give you the desires of your heart."

This section of the book will provide you with uplifting stories; both personal and biblical, to encourage you to walk with the faith of God in your life so that you can live a victorious life. Whether you are seeking God for faith, healing, hope, joy, peace, prosperity, trust, or wisdom, God will come through for you in every aspect of life. 2 Timothy 4:7 (NIV) says, "I have fought the good fight, I have finished the race, I have kept the faith." Let that scripture penetrate your heart as you run your race.

TESTIMONY OF FAITH

The Bible says in Matthew 17:20 (NIV), "If you have faith as small as a mustard seed, you can say to this mountain, 'Move from here to there,' and it will move. Nothing will be impossible for you." Sometimes we get so wrapped up in our lives and the circumstances that surround us that we forget that without faith, it is impossible to please God. Therefore, if your faith is only as small as a mustard seed, then that is all you need.

That reminds me of a story. In 2018, I was listening to a podcast by Terri Savelle Foy about how she paid off her swimming pool. Her testimony encouraged me so much that I thought to myself, *If Terri can pay off her swimming pool, then my husband and I can pay off our land.* We sought God and planted a financial seed in church. I reminded God that He was no respecter of persons (Acts 10:34 KJV). I said to God, "If you can pay off Terri's swimming pool then you can help us pay off our land." In February 2019, God made a way and we were able to pay off our land. Glory to God! Whatever you are believing God to help you through, keep walking by faith, thanking God for His goodness, and trust Him as it is manifested in your life.

One of my friends in Florida shared a testimony based on Proverbs 3:5–6 (NLT). "Trust in the Lord with all your heart; do not depend on your own understanding. Seek His will in all you do, and He will show you which path to take." She said:

> Out of all the scriptures from my 30-Days "Faith Scriptures" of Scripture Script, this one touched my heart. I was going through some challenges with the closing requirements for my new home, to the point that I thought I was not going to be able to close on my new home. After reading this scripture, I knew in my heart that our God is faithful and that although I did not see it, He was working everything out. I just needed to "keep my faith" and have patience while waiting on Him. The following week, July 1, 2020, was the closing of our new home, and everything had fallen into place just the way God planned it for me and my family." (Nina Ramirez of Florida)

Biblical Testimonies of Faith

A wonderful story in the Bible to build your faith is found in Matthew 8:5–13 (NLT). It says:

> When Jesus returned to Capernaum, a Roman officer came and pleaded with Him, "Lord, my young servant

lies in bed, paralyzed and in terrible pain." Jesus said, "I will come and heal him." But the officer said, "Lord, I am not worthy to have you come into my home. Just say the word from where you are, and my servant will be healed. I know this because I am under the authority of my superior officers, and I have authority over my soldiers. I only need to say, 'Go,' and they go, or 'Come,' and they come. And if I say to my slaves, 'Do this,' they do it." When Jesus heard this, He was amazed. Turning to those who were following Him, He said, "I tell you the truth, I haven't seen faith like this in all Israel! And I tell you this, that many Gentiles will come from all over the world—from east and west—and sit down with Abraham, Isaac, and Jacob at the feast in the Kingdom of Heaven. But many Israelites— those for whom the Kingdom was prepared—will be thrown into outer darkness, where there will be weeping and gnashing of teeth." Then Jesus said to the Roman officer, "Go back home. Because you believed, it has happened." And the young servant was healed that same hour."

This story demonstrates that having faith captures the attention of God. I want to leave you with one more scripture to energize your spirit. "Then Jesus told them, "I tell you the truth, if you have faith and don't doubt, you can do things like this and much more. You can even say to this mountain, 'May you be lifted up and thrown into the sea,' and it will happen" (Matt. 21:21 NLT).

TESTIMONIES OF HEALING

The Bible says in Psalms 107:19–21 (NIV):

> Then they cried to the Lord in their
> trouble, and He saved them from
> their distress. He sent out His word
> and healed them; He rescued them
> from the grave. Let them give thanks
> to the Lord for His unfailing love and
> His wonderful deeds for mankind.

What a testimony of God's goodness. He sent His Word and healed them. What kind of healing do you need? God wants you to be healed physically, mentally, emotionally, and spiritually. Psalm 34:17–20 (NLT) says:

> The Lord hears his people when
> they call to Him for help. He rescues
> them from all their troubles. The
> Lord is close to the brokenhearted;
> He rescues those whose spirits are
> crushed. The righteous person
> faces many troubles, but the Lord
> comes to the rescue each time. For
> the Lord protects the bones of the
> righteous; not one of them is broken!

This reminds me of a story that occurred on December 16, 2004. I had just picked up some pictures that were developed at a local drug store in the small town where my husband and family lived. I was on my way to pick up our two youngest children from elementary school. As I approached the intersection of the school, I saw an ambulance and a child lying on the ground. My heart sunk! I saw the coat and knew instantly it was one of our children. I threw the car door open and ran up to our son. I stood over the top of him calling him by name and evaluating him neurologically. I was told that our son was running across the street when he was hit by a truck. Instantly, I began praying over him. Our son was placed on the stretcher and lifted up into the ambulance. God gave me favor that day with the ambulance crew. I was allowed to enter the ambulance and sit at the side of our son as we both traveled to the hospital.

My brother-in-law took my car home and my husband met me at the local hospital. As we arrived, my husband and I prayed together over our son that God would heal him. We prayed that our son would have no injuries, deficits, or broken bones. Our son's pastor arrived and he prayed with us as well. Additionally, many friends and family in the community and our church were praying for our son. My husband and I believed God's Word and trusted Him that our son was healed.

After the imaging exams were completed and the physician had evaluated our son, we were told that he would need to stay in the hospital overnight to be evaluated for a head injury. Our son had a significant amount of swelling to his face and several lacerations on his face that needed repair. No further injuries or broken bones were identified. We were able to take our son home the next day. We did have to follow-up medically for a year after the event to make sure there were not any deficits or setbacks with walking. Our son was released after one year.

Biblical Testimonies of Healing

I want to reflect on two different accounts of healing where Jesus healed a woman and a daughter. Both stories are found in Luke 8:40–55 (ESV). It says:

> Now when Jesus returned, the crowd
> welcomed Him, for they were all
> waiting for Him. And there came
> a man named Jairus, who was a
> ruler of the synagogue. And falling
> at Jesus' feet, he implored Him to
> come to his house, for he had an only
> daughter, about twelve years of age,
> and she was dying. As Jesus went,
> the people pressed around Him. And
> there was a woman who had had a
> discharge of blood for twelve years,
> and though she had spent all her
> living on physicians, she could not
> be healed by anyone. She came up
> behind Him and touched the fringe
> of His garment, and immediately
> her discharge of blood ceased. And

Jesus said, "Who was it that touched me?" When all denied it, Peter said, "Master, the crowds surround you and are pressing in on you!" But Jesus said, "Someone touched me, for I perceive that power has gone out from me." And when the woman saw that she was not hidden, she came trembling, and falling down before Him declared in the presence of all the people why she had touched Him, and how she had been immediately healed. And He said to her, "Daughter, your faith has made you well; go in peace." While He was still speaking, someone from the ruler's house came and said, "Your daughter is dead; do not trouble the Teacher any more." But Jesus on hearing this answered him, "Do not fear; only believe, and she will be well." And when He came to the house, He allowed no one to enter with him, except Peter and John and James, and the father and mother of the child. And all were weeping and mourning for her, but He said, "Do not weep, for she is not dead but sleeping." And they laughed at Him, knowing that she was dead. But taking her by the hand He called, saying, "Child, arise." And her spirit returned, and she got up at once.

In the first account, the woman bled for twelve years spending everything she had and doing everything within her own power. All natural hope was gone as no one could heal her. She was desperate and when she saw Jesus, all her focus and faith was on the belief that if she could touch a fringe of His garment, she would be healed. She was so determined that she put herself out on a limb to receive her healing from Jesus. Jesus healed her because of her great faith. Are you this person in the story? Are you so desperate that you are willing to get focused on God and believe His Word to obtain your healing? It took this woman twelve years of trying everything in her natural ability to get her healing. If you ask God to heal you and you don't see the manifestation in the natural, don't give up. Keep believing. Keep trusting. Keep your faith in the Word of God. The Bible tells us in 2 Corinthians 5:7 (NIV), "For we live by faith, not by sight."

In the second account, Jairus pleaded his case with Jesus. He was focused on Jesus going to his house to heal his twelve-year-old daughter. Jesus agreed and had every intention to heal Jairus's daughter. While on the way to his house, other circumstances delayed the journey and Jairus received news that his daughter had died. Jesus heard the news and instantly told Jairus to not be afraid, believe, and his daughter would be healed. Other people's unbelief tried to creep in so Jairus would give up. Jairus traveled with Jesus and when they arrived at his home, only people with faith were allowed in the daughter's room. Jesus spoke to the daughter and she awakened.

These stories remind me of life. As we are believing God for anything including healing; distractions and doubt can get in our way and try to get us off the path of believing and trusting in God. We have to press in and stand on the Word of God. Just as Jesus told Jairus to not be afraid but believe and his daughter will be healed, we have to do that. Even if people around you laugh and mock you, stand your ground, keep the faith, trust God, and thank Him until that which you are believing Him for is manifested in your life.

TESTIMONIES OF HOPE

While looking back on my life, I can see now how God perfectly coordinated my life to fulfill the desires of my heart. Honestly, while going through all the life challenges of growing up, developing a relationship with my biological father whom I discovered at the age of twelve, going to college, marrying the man of my dreams, and having a large family, I didn't know if I was ever going to be able to pursue a career as a registered nurse. I had always hoped that one day the desire of my heart would come to pass but, I just didn't know if I could do it. Doubt would creep in as I would think about the words of my high school counselor who told me that I would never be able to become a nurse because my grades weren't good enough.

When doubt creeps in, we have to defeat the devil by speaking the Word of God over our lives. James 4:7 (NIV) says, "Submit yourselves, then, to God. Resist the devil, and he will flee from you." When God sets into us such a strong knowing or a desire into our heart, we can't let the negative words of people derail us from our passions. When people speak negativity, their words don't affect them (although they are probably unhappy people) but it does affect us if we allow it to. For example: if David had listened to man, he would not have had victory over Goliath. If Noah listened to logic, the ark would not have been built. If Joseph would have listened to his brothers, he would have missed the blessings of

God in his life and his family may have starved. We need to remember what Philippians 4:8 (NIV) says:

> Finally, brothers and sisters,
> whatever is true, whatever is noble,
> whatever is right, whatever is
> pure, whatever is lovely, whatever
> is admirable—if anything is
> excellent or praiseworthy—
> think about such things.

Thinking and declaring good things over our lives will give us opportunities to share the victories of what we once thought was impossible but God made it possible.

Have Faith, Believe and Keep the Hope

While in the hospital in September 1995 after delivering my fourth child, my husband looked over at me and asked, "When are you going to pursue your nursing career? You know that is what you've always wanted to do." That tugged at my heart and we began having conversations about returning to college. Of course, I knew it was not going to be easy but I had a husband who loved me and supported me. He encouraged and nurtured me in every way possible. I also recognized that God loves me and He believed in me, otherwise I wouldn't have had the desire in my life to be an obstetrical nurse.

God worked out all of the details for me to return to college and in January 1997, while pregnant with our fifth child, I returned to college taking night classes to complete some of the required courses before entering the nursing program. Not only did I return to college, but so did my husband. We both returned together taking classes towards pursuing nursing degrees.

Keep your hope in God knowing that He is faithful. God knows the end from the beginning and knows how everything is going to work out. I applied for a non-traditional scholarship and was chosen by a couple who had no children. They wanted to provide a scholarship to a student who was trying to further their education with a family. Excitedly, I received a full-ride scholarship that included tuition, fees, and books. In December of 1999, I completed all the requirements for the nursing program. I took the NCLEX nursing exam in January 2000 and received notification in the mail of passing the exam on February 14, 2000. My husband completed all his requirements as well and passed the NCLEX nursing exam in the summer of 2004.

Biblical Testimonies of Hope

What are you hoping for? The Bible tells us in Proverbs 13:12 (NIV), "Hope deferred makes the heart sick, but a longing fulfilled is a tree of life." Hope gives us the reason to continue especially when we find ourselves in the lonely valleys of life. Ephesians 1:18 (NLT) says, "I pray that your hearts will be flooded with light so that you can understand the confident hope He has given to those He called—His holy people who are His rich and glorious inheritance." Let's read this story in Luke 15:11–24 (NIV), where a father could have given up on his child but he kept his hope and trust in God. Jesus was speaking parables to the tax collectors, sinners, Pharisees, and teachers: He said beginning in verse 11:

There was a man who had two sons. The younger one said to his father, 'Father, give me my share of the estate.' So he divided his property between them. Not long after that, the younger son got together all he had, set off for a distant country and there squandered his wealth in wild living. After he had spent everything, there was a severe famine in that whole country, and he began to be in need. So he went and hired himself out to a citizen of that country, who sent him to his fields to feed pigs. He longed to fill his stomach with the pods that the pigs were eating, but no one gave him anything. When he came to his senses, he said, 'How many of my father's hired servants have food to spare, and here I am starving to death! I will set out and go back to my father and say to him: Father, I have sinned against

heaven and against you. I am no
longer worthy to be called your
son; make me like one of your hired
servants.' So he got up and went
to his father. But while he was still
a long way off, his father saw him
and was filled with compassion for
him; he ran to his son, threw his
arms around him and kissed him.
The son said to him, 'Father, I have
sinned against heaven and against
you. I am no longer worthy to be
called your son.' But the father said
to his servants, 'Quick! Bring the
best robe and put it on him. Put a
ring on his finger and sandals on his
feet. Bring the fattened calf and kill
it. Let's have a feast and celebrate.
For this son of mine was dead and is
alive again; he was lost and is found.'

After reading this story, you may say the son was irre-
sponsible as he spent all of his wealth on foolish living. We
cannot disagree with that, but, when the son hit rock bottom, he came to his senses and decided to return home.
The joy the father must have experienced was euphoric as
he saw his son off in the distance, returning home. The
father held nothing against his son. He returned him to
full sonship and all authority and riches of the family.

As a parent, this story shows the overwhelming example of hope as the father and son were again united. I pray this story encourages you to keep hoping with earnest expectation until the manifestation of what you are believing God for occurs in your life.

TESTIMONY OF JOY

The Bible says in Psalm 16:11 (NIV), "You make known to me the path of life; you will fill me with joy in your presence, with eternal pleasures at your right hand." In the midst of our daily commitments, schedules, and duties, we can be thankful with a joyful heart for all that God has done. Romans 15:13 (NLT) says, "I pray that God, the source of hope, will fill you completely with joy and peace because you trust in Him. Then you will overflow with confident hope through the power of the Holy Spirit."

A married couple my husband and I know in Florida, share a testimony of joy as they stood on the Word of God to move back home.

> God grants us joy for the journey. This joy is not the type of joy that's known to man, but a heavenly joy that the Bible describes as unspeakable and full of glory. During our years in Bible school, the Lord taught us faith, unlike anything we had ever learned before. We saw the hand of God upon our lives in amazing ways, but there was one particular time in our lives when we had to step out in faith and that left a lasting footprint in my heart.

Although we lived by faith and walked by faith, this particular event was different for some reason. Before packing up and heading out from Miami, Florida to Tulsa, Oklahoma, for Bible school, we had our first boy. Eight years later the Lord instructed us to return home to Miami. We faced a challenge, however, because we left Miami with one child, but was heading back with three boys. It was easy moving to Tulsa because our boy was just a baby. We just strapped his car seat in the middle of a one-row seat moving truck, hitched our car in the back, and headed for Tulsa. The challenge, however, was heading back. We had our belongings to bring back with us as a family of five. With a specific budget to work with, our options were narrowing down quickly. There were no moving trucks with a back-row seat to load our boys. Besides it going beyond our budget, my wife refused to fly out with our kids and leave me behind to drive a huge moving truck for twenty-two hours alone. Shipping our belongings surpassed our budget and time was quickly running out.

After exhausting our options, I began to search my spirit for guidance. It is interesting how we hear from God to do something, but often we forget to stay plugged into Him for guidance in the full plan. I picked up in my spirit to have my wife search for a rental pickup truck that would provide a back row of seats for our boys and that had a hitch in the back that could pull a cargo with our belongings. It sounded perfect and it would fit our budget. The entire family will comfortably fit in the rental pickup truck, our belongings will be hitched up to the back and we'll have our car shipped to Miami.

There was, however, one problem. My dear wife searched tirelessly, night after night, for an auto rental company that would rent a pickup truck with back seats available and a hitch in the back for cargo. To our disappointment, we found out that rent-a-car companies forbade towing in the back of their vehicles. We searched every company there was, but each one was clear about not towing. What seemed like an easy task became difficult.

At this time the Lord began to permeate from within me a peace beyond human comprehension. Such peace was accompanied with a supernatural joy that provided me with supernatural strength for the journey. The Lord placed in my heart the scripture, "The Lord will perfect that which concerneth me: thy mercy, O Lord, endureth for ever. Forsake not the works of thine own hands" (Ps. 138:8 KJV). This scripture became stronger and stronger in my heart. Every time I thought about the problem, I said out of my spirit, "The Lord will perfect that which concerns me." I'd be in the shower saying, "The Lord will perfect that which concerns me." While driving down the highway saying, "The Lord will perfect that which concerns me." While spending time with family and friends I would say, "The Lord will perfect that which concerns me." I'd go to bed and wake up saying, "The Lord will perfect that which concerns me." Every time the thought came to my mind that it seemed impossible to move, I'd say, "The Lord will perfect that which concerns me." Day and night I'd speak out from my spirit, "The Lord will perfect that which concerns me." When the devil whispered doubt and discouragement to me, I'd say, "The Lord will perfect that which concerns me." Every time I said it, faith grew stronger and joy was present.

Well, the day came when our notice to leave our apartment in Tulsa was present. We had packed all of our belongings and without any plan B to fall back on, just solely one plan, one will, a Word from God that said to rent a vehicle and the Word of God that says, "The Lord will perfect that which concerns me." My wife had reserved a pickup truck with back seats for the kids except it had no hitch to load cargo for our belongings. Needless to say, I had still reserved a trailer with U-Haul in pure faith. This cargo would obviously need a vehicle with a towing hitch to pull it. I had arranged with a friend of ours to give me a ride to the car rental company. Upon arriving, I noticed a nice clean pickup truck parked outside the rental office and so I stretched my neck to look at the back of the vehicle only to see there wasn't a hitch. My friend dropped me off and asked if I needed her to wait for me. I said, "No, I'll be fine," and off she went. I walked into the rental office and the associate asked if I was here to pick up my keys. I replied, "Yes, but sir, do you have any other trucks on the lot?" The gentleman said, "No, can I check you out?" I kept declaring to myself, "The Lord will perfect that which concerns me" and continued to question the man, "Sir are you sure there isn't another truck on the lot that I could look at?" Out of frustration, the man said, "Yes, there is one truck parked in the back of the lot, but it is not to be rented." I said, "Sir, can I see the truck?" Becoming impatient, the man said to me, "Sir, there is no reason to see the other vehicle because there was a problem obtaining the registration so it does not have a registration." I persisted and out of frustration the associate finally agreed to show me the other vehicle. Meanwhile, I'm still confessing, "The Lord will perfect that which concerns me." When I approached the vehicle that had no registration for rental, I stretched my neck beneath the back of the vehicle, and lo and behold the truck had a big hitch hooked up on the back end for towing. I said, "Sir, I want this vehicle." The man said, "It's not clean and there is no registration for the vehicle!"

As we made our way back inside and the associate was going to check out the initial vehicle that was originally reserved for me, I kept saying, "The Lord will perfect that which concerns me." Meanwhile, my family was waiting at the apartment, filled with boxes and no physical evidence for our move to Miami. Just before checking me out, the man froze and his eyes became large. He looked up at me and said, "Sir, I don't understand it, but the title for the other truck just came into the system." In shock and uncertainty, he mumbled, "Do you still want the other truck?" I said, "The Lord perfects that which concerns me… Yes, sir, I will take the truck!" That day with joy and gladness, I drove over to a U-Haul shop, hooked up my trailer to the hitch of the rental truck, and drove to our apartment with my horn honking. Bless God, my family came running outside shouting, "You got it! You got it!" You got it!"

My friend, the Lord had perfected that which concerned me and my family. God's joy never ceased to end during that event in our lives. He secured our joy, sustained our strength, and kept His word. The Lord perfected what concerned me and my family and He will perfect that which concerns you. So keep your song of victory, stay grounded in the Word of God, keep the switch of faith turned on, and remain in the joy of the Lord because it is your strength. Hallelujah!" (Sean and Natacha Kalicharan of Florida).

Biblical Testimonies of Joy

The Bible says in 1 Peter 1:8–9 (NIV):

Though you have not seen Him,
you love Him; and even though you
do not see Him now, you believe
in Him and are filled with an
inexpressible and glorious joy, for you
are receiving the end result of your
faith, the salvation of your souls.

As shown in that scripture, joy is a direct correlation to our salvation of Jesus Christ. Through the gift of salvation, the Holy Spirit "produces this kind of fruit in our lives: love, joy, peace, patience, kindness, goodness, faithfulness, gentleness, and self-control. There is no law against these things!" (Gal. 5:22–23 NLT). Let's read a story found in Matthew 2:1–11 (ESV), which brought joy to the earth the night of our Lord and Savior's birth.

> Now after Jesus was born in Bethlehem of Judea in the days of Herod the king, behold, wise men from the east came to Jerusalem, saying, "Where is He who has been born king of the Jews? For we saw His star when it rose and have come to worship Him." When Herod the king heard this, he was troubled, and all Jerusalem with him; and assembling all the chief priests and scribes of the people, he inquired of them where the Christ was to be born. They told him, "In Bethlehem of Judea, for so it is written by the prophet: "'And you, O Bethlehem, in the land of Judah, are by no means least among the rulers of Judah; for from you shall come a ruler who will shepherd my people Israel.'"
>
> Then Herod summoned the wise men secretly and ascertained from them what time the star had appeared. And he sent them to Bethlehem, saying, "Go and search

diligently for the child, and when you have found him, bring me word, that I too may come and worship Him." After listening to the king, they went on their way. And behold, the star that they had seen when it rose went before them until it came to rest over the place where the child was. When they saw the star, they rejoiced exceedingly with great joy. And going into the house, they saw the child with Mary His mother, and they fell down and worshiped Him. Then, opening their treasures, they offered Him gifts, gold and frankincense and myrrh.

Through the above story, we can see that our hearts should be full of joy through the salvation of our Lord and Savior Jesus Christ. "May the God of hope fill you with all joy and peace as you trust in Him, so that you may overflow with hope by the power of the Holy Spirit" (Rom. 15:13 NIV).

TESTIMONIES OF PEACE

God desires that we live with peace in our life. Isaiah 26:3 (NIV) says, "You will keep in perfect peace those whose minds are steadfast, because they trust in you." As we remain in fellowship with Him and stay devoted to the Word of God, "then you will experience God's peace, which exceeds anything we can understand. His peace will guard your hearts and minds as you live in Christ Jesus." Philippians 4:7 (NLT). My niece and her husband share a testimony of peace as they stand together on the Word of God believing in the manifestation of healing in their life.

During the year 2020, we have seen God's comfort of peace in our hearts when it has seemed overwhelming. My husband was diagnosed with a panic disorder when we were engaged in 2014, which has come back through a few seasons in our marriage including at the beginning of 2020. I admit it is far too tough to sit in the presence of my husband when he is suffering beyond words at the height of a panic attack. But, we are grateful for these moments of utter dependence on our Heavenly Father for comfort, when all we can do is pray for His closeness. My husband hasn't been healed miraculously of his anxiety, but when we have weathered other struggles, we are reminded of how God has been sufficient before and will be again, and in that, we can have peace.

We frequently go to the book of Ephesians, chapter 6, where Paul writes how to use God's armor as protection to stay strong. I have found great peace and comfort when He repeats in verse 13 (NIV), "and after you have done everything, to stand." God is aware of the struggles we have and as He clearly describes, if after everything else, to just stand. That's it. When I am overwhelmed by situations far past my capacity to fix or overcome, I can just stand in His presence and trust in His promise. It doesn't mean life will be pain-free or easy, but I have confidence that our God has overcome it already. In keeping our eyes on the outcome already foretold, we can have peace in His sovereignty." (Eric and Bekah Huebschman of Wisconsin)

Biblical Testimonies of Peace

The Bible tells us in Isaiah 9:6 that Jesus is the prince of peace. Jesus wants us to walk out our life with peace. John 16:33 (NIV) says, "I have told you these things, so that in me you may have peace. In this world you will have trouble. But take heart! I have overcome the world." How glorious is that scripture? God never promised us a life without difficulty, challenges or obstacles but, in all of it, we can live in peace. Let's look at a story in

Matthew 8:23–27 (NLT) where Jesus calmed the storms and provided peace to those who were with Him.

> Then Jesus got into the boat and started across the lake with His disciples. Suddenly, a fierce storm struck the lake, with waves breaking into the boat. But Jesus was sleeping. The disciples went and woke Him up, shouting, "Lord, save us! We're going to drown!" Jesus responded, "Why are you afraid? You have so little faith!" Then He got up and rebuked the wind and waves, and suddenly there was a great calm. The disciples were amazed. "Who is this man?" they asked. "Even the winds and waves obey Him!"

So, through this story, we can apply the same principle in our life as children of God. When you are challenged with the storms of life, speak to your situation just as Jesus did. Declare over your life Mark 4:39 (ESV), "Peace! Be still!" As you do this and keep your eyes focused on God, watch Him calm the wind and storms in your life.

TESTIMONIES OF FINANCIAL PROSPERITY

The Word of God tells us in Psalm 23:10 (NLT), "The Lord is my shepherd; I have all that I need." That clearly says that we should not lack in any area of life. It also says in Philippians 4:19 (NIV), "And my God will meet all your needs according to the riches of His glory in Christ Jesus." A friend who lives in Florida shared a testimony of how God taught her to trust Him with her finances.

> In 2003, my husband decided to refinance our mortgage to a fifteen-year mortgage. This almost doubled our payment. It took all his disability payment and some of my paycheck to make the payment each month. But we managed to make it every month on time.
>
> Then in 2007, my husband died and left me with this huge mortgage payment. Because he had been diabetic, he could not get life insurance. I lost his disability payments and because I was now single, the company I worked for took an additional $300 a month out of my pay. It was rough going. I did everything I could to cut costs. I could not afford to sell the house because

of the refinancing, I didn't have very much equity to start over. I managed the best I could. I was late a few times with the mortgage. Some months I paid the electric bill and some months I paid the water bill.

I have been a Christian for many years. Many times, over the years, I have listened to sermons that taught me that the best way out of financial setbacks is to keep tithing and giving. I was never late on my tithes or my offerings. I knew it was the only way out and I believed God's Word. He said He would never leave me nor forsake me (Deut.31:6 NIV).

In November 2008, I had a few unexpected expenses, and I did not have enough money to pay my mortgage. I did not know what to do. I kept meditating on Isaiah 41:10 (NKJV), "Fear not, for I am with you." I did not want to ask to borrow money from family or friends. As a tither, I know Malachi 3:10 (KJV), "Bring ye all the tithes into the storehouse, that there may be meat in mine house, and prove me now herewith, saith the LORD of hosts, if I will not open you the windows of heaven, and pour you out a blessing, that there shall not be room enough to receive it." God said to prove Him. I took my stand that God was true to His word.

I started praying in the Spirit about the situation. I heard the Holy Spirit tell me to have the mortgage company pay my mortgage. I thought, "That's crazy, God, the mortgage company isn't going to pay my mortgage, I'm supposed to pay them!" But God's mind cannot be changed so I finally picked up my cell phone to call the mortgage company. As I started to dial the number, I remembered that my escrow account had extra money in it. The first person that answered, I told her I was a widow, and I did not have enough money to pay the mortgage this month and could they take the payment out of my escrow account? She was sweet and said she thought that could happen. I was so relieved! She transferred me to a different department. While I was waiting for them to answer, I was pacing the bedroom and praying in the Spirit. Another lady picked up and I had to explain all over again that I did not have money to pay the mortgage and could it be taken out of my escrow account? She also said that it should not be a problem, but she had to transfer me to another department. I again was pacing the bedroom and praying in the Spirit. This time a man answered, and I had to repeat my request again. When I was finished, he very brusquely said, "No, that money is only for taxes and insurance."

Somewhere inside me, a boldness came up and I said, "I would like to speak to your supervisor." He was silent for a moment and then asked me to hang on. So, I paced the bedroom again praying in the Spirit. I was beginning to think he hung up on me. About twenty minutes later he was back on the phone and said, "Not only will we pay your mortgage but all your late fees as well."

All I could do was jump around the bedroom praising God and shouting, "Hallelujah!" I was never late on another mortgage payment!" (Linda Berry of Florida)

Biblical Testimonies of Prosperity

The Bible tells the story of a widow woman who was in desperate need of God's help. When her husband died, he left her with debt and the loaner wanted his money. Have you been in this situation where you owed money to someone and they wanted their money? Maybe it was a bank, family member, friend, or neighbor. Let's read a story in 2 Kings 4:1–7 (CEV) to see how God made a way for this woman.

> One day, the widow of one of the Lord's prophets said to Elisha, "You know that before my husband died, he was a follower of yours and a worshiper of the Lord. But he owed a man some money, and now that man is on his way to take my two sons as his slaves." "Maybe there's something I can do to help," Elisha said. "What do you have in your house?" "Sir, I have nothing but a small bottle of olive oil." Elisha told her, "Ask your neighbors for their empty jars. And after you've borrowed as many as you can, go home and shut the door behind you and your sons. Then begin filling the jars with oil and set each one aside as you fill it." The woman left. Later, when she and her sons were back inside their

house, the two sons brought her
the jars, and she began filling them.
At last, she said to one of her sons,
"Bring me another jar." "We don't
have any more," he answered, and
the oil stopped flowing from the
small bottle. After she told Elisha
what had happened, he said, "Sell
the oil and use part of the money to
pay what you owe the man. You and
your sons can live on what is left."

That story is a great testimony of how God took
something the woman already had available in her hands,
added grace and favor, then miraculously intervened to
provide financial provision to her and her family. Just
like the story, if you are left in a financial need, seek
God so He can reveal to you what needs to be done in
your situation. I want to leave you with a few scriptures
to encourage you as you're believing God for financial
provision.

Then the Lord your God will make
you most prosperous in all the
work of your hands and in the fruit
of your womb, the young of your
livestock and the crops of your land.
The Lord will again delight in you
and make you prosperous, just as
He delighted in your ancestors.
Deuteronomy 30:9 (NIV)

"My help comes from the Lord, who made heaven and earth" (Ps. 121:2 ESV).

"A man's gift makes room for him and brings him before great men" (Prov. 18:16 NASB).

"Seek the Kingdom of God above all else, and live righteously, and He will give you everything you need" (Matt. 6:33 NLT).

"Beloved, I pray that in all respects you may prosper and be in good health, just as your soul prospers" (3 John 1:2 NASB).

Give to others, and God will give to you. Indeed, you will receive a full measure, a generous helping, poured into your hands—all that you can hold. The measure you use for others is the one that God will use for you.

Luke 6:38 (GNT)

TESTIMONIES OF FAITH, THANKFULNESS, AND TRUST

Have you ever been in a situation where God asked you to do something and you just didn't know if you could do it? At the beginning of 2020, I was working on the legal side of setting up my ministry. I had a list of things I needed to accomplish and didn't know how I was going to do it all. I was seeking God diligently for direction so the legal part of the ministry would be set up how He wanted me to establish it. I remember one day as I was praying, I was in tears and cried out to God. I told Him that I am overwhelmed and just didn't know how to do everything. The presence of God surrounded me and in my spirit, I could see Jesus putting His hand on my left shoulder and said, "It is okay, Connie, we are going to do it together step by step." I was so relieved and at peace. Every morning while I was in prayer, God would tell me exactly what I needed to do that day. I put my faith and trust in God and every day completed the tasks as instructed in prayer. The legal side of the ministry was completed and I was able to launch "Living in the Light Women's Ministry International, LLC" on March 1, 2020.

Biblical Testimonies of Faith, Thankfulness, and Trust

Let's read a story in Acts 9:1–18 (NIV) that demonstrated the faith of Ananias, thankfulness, and trust in God while he carried out the instructions of the Lord.

Meanwhile, Saul was still breathing out murderous threats against the Lord's disciples. He went to the high priest and asked him for letters to the synagogues in Damascus, so that if he found any there who belonged to the Way, whether men or women, he might take them as prisoners to Jerusalem. As he neared Damascus on his journey, suddenly a light from heaven flashed around him. He fell to the ground and heard a voice say to him, "Saul, Saul, why do you persecute me?" "Who are you, Lord?" Saul asked. "I am Jesus, whom you are persecuting," He replied. "Now get up and go into the city, and you will be told what you must do." The men traveling with Saul stood there speechless; they heard the sound but did not see anyone. Saul got up from the ground, but when he opened his eyes he could see nothing. So they led him by the hand into Damascus. For three days he was blind and did not eat or drink anything.

In Damascus, there was a disciple named Ananias. The Lord called to him in a vision, "Ananias!" "Yes, Lord," he answered. The Lord told him, "Go to the house of Judas on Straight Street and ask for a man from Tarsus named Saul, for he is praying. In a vision he has seen a man named Ananias come and place his hands on him to restore his sight." "Lord," Ananias answered, "I have heard many reports about this man and all the harm he has done to your holy people in Jerusalem. And he has come here with authority from the chief priests to arrest all who call on your name." But the Lord said to Ananias, "Go! This man is my chosen instrument to proclaim my name to the Gentiles and their kings and to the people of Israel. I will show him how much he must suffer for my name." Then Ananias went to the house and entered it. Placing his hands on Saul, he said, "Brother Saul, the Lord— Jesus, who appeared to you on the road as you were coming here—has sent me so that you may see again and be filled with the Holy Spirit." Immediately, something like scales fell from Saul's eyes, and he could see again.

I can't imagine the different thoughts that must have been going through Ananias's mind when the Lord instructed Ananias through a vision to "go to the house of Judas," and pray for Saul so his sight would be restored and be filled with the Holy Spirit. Ananias had concerns that he discussed with the Lord but through Ananias's faith and trust in the Lord, he did what was requested. I am sure Ananias was very relieved and thankful that he was not arrested and placed in prison after fulfilling the request of the Lord.

Let's read another story where a man was made whole because of his thankfulness. Luke 17:11–19 (NIV) says:

> Now on His way to Jerusalem, Jesus traveled along the border between Samaria and Galilee. As He was going into a village, ten men who had leprosy met Him. They stood at a distance and called out in a loud voice, "Jesus, Master, have pity on us!" When He saw them, He said, "Go, show yourselves to the priests." And as they went, they were cleansed. One of them, when he saw he was healed, came back, praising God in a loud voice. He threw himself at Jesus' feet and thanked Him—and he was a Samaritan. Jesus asked, "Were not all ten cleansed? Where are the other nine? Has no one returned to give praise to God except this foreigner?" Then He said to him, "Rise and go; your faith has made you well."

Through both of these stories, it shows us the importance of walking in faith, trusting God, and having a thankful heart that if God has asked us to do something, the provision will be there.

TESTIMONIES OF WISDOM

We can all use the wisdom of God to operate in our life. The Bible says in James 1:5 (NIV), "If any of you lacks wisdom, you should ask God, who gives generously to all without finding fault, and it will be given to you." Proverbs 4:11 (NIV) says, "I instruct you in the way of wisdom and lead you along straight paths." My husband and I stood on these scriptures. We would like to share a story of how the wisdom of God directed us in our life to pay off the extra land that we purchased when we bought our home in Florida.

In 2018, while in prayer, God spoke to me and told me I needed to learn how to manage my finances. I heeded this directive and we started learning as much as we could about finances. Les and I worked diligently to get out of debt. We followed the "Baby Steps" according to Dave Ramsey's plan. The only debt left was our home and the land that we purchased when we bought the home. We had been planting financial seed and believing God to pay off our land.

We read the Bible and meditated on the following three scriptures: 3 John 1:2 (KJV), "Beloved, I wish above all things that thou mayest prosper and be in health, even as thy soul prospereth." Proverbs 3:13 (NIV), "Blessed are those who find wisdom, those who gain understanding." Lastly, Proverbs 18:20 (TPT), "The spiritually hungry are always ready to learn more, for their hearts are eager to discover new truths." Through learning and gaining knowledge in the area of finances, it provided Les and me with more wisdom in financial decision making.

In November 2018, while in prayer, God spoke to me and told me to sell stock that had nothing to do with any of our retirement accounts. I had never done that before and started learning as much as I could to make that transaction. Les and I were watching the stock market and increasing our knowledge. We decided on an amount and we waited for the opportunity to sell. I even did a practice trial run to see how it worked along with watching videos on how to sell the stock. The stock never reached the amount that Les and I had agreed on so we never sold the stock. Then the stock prices dropped. My heart sunk because I felt like I missed God. I remember repenting and telling God I was sorry for not selling the stock but I struggled with the fact that I didn't have a release in my spirit to sell. I thought that maybe I was being too greedy on the agreed amount. I asked God to give us another chance.

Then in February 2019, while in prayer, God spoke to me this time and said to sell my stock. He told me that the stock prices were going to drop and would be down for several months. Les and I prayed, came into agreement and within three weeks we sold a portion of my stock, doubled our money, and we were able to pay off our land in full. It was incredible to think that the balance we paid off was almost the same cost as the first home we bought back in 1991. Les and I were so excited to see God move in our life through His wisdom, instruction, and provision.

Biblical Testimonies of Wisdom

The Bible tells us in James 1:5 (NIV), "If any of you lacks wisdom, you should ask God, who gives generously to all without finding fault, and it will be given to you." It is imperative that in this day and age that we walk out our lives with the wisdom of God to avoid the pitfalls in life. Let's read about King Solomon in the Bible and see what he said to God in 1 Kings 3: 4–14 (MSG) regarding wisdom.

> The king went to Gibeon, the most prestigious of the local shrines, to worship. He sacrificed a thousand Whole-Burnt-Offerings on that altar. That night, there in Gibeon, God appeared to Solomon in a dream: God said, "What can I give you? Ask." Solomon said, "You were extravagantly generous in love with David my father, and he lived faithfully in your presence, his relationships were just and his heart right. And you have persisted in this great and generous love by giving him—and this very day!—a son to sit on his throne.
>
> And now here I am: GOD, my God, you have made me, your servant, ruler of the kingdom in

place of David my father. I'm too
young for this, a mere child! I don't
know the ropes, hardly know the
'ins' and 'outs' of this job. And here
I am, set down in the middle of
the people you've chosen, a great
people—far too many to ever count.

Here's what I want: Give me a God-
listening heart so I can lead your
people well, discerning the difference
between good and evil. For who
on their own is capable of leading
your glorious people?" God, the
Master, was delighted with Solomon's
response. And God said to him,
"Because you have asked for this and
haven't grasped after a long life, or
riches, or the doom of your enemies,
but you have asked for the ability to
lead and govern well, I'll give you
what you've asked for—I'm giving
you a wise and mature heart. There's
never been one like you before; and
there'll be no one after. As a bonus,
I'm giving you both the wealth and
glory you didn't ask for—there's not
a king anywhere who will come up to
your mark. And if you stay on course,
keeping your eye on the life-map and

the God-signs as your father David did, I'll also give you a long life."

We can see that through this story, King Solomon wanted a God-listening heart so he could lead and govern his people. King Solomon had a great responsibility in his life as a young man to be a good steward over his father's kingdom. He recognized the need for help and instead of asking for riches, King Solomon needed godly wisdom. Let me emphasize the following scripture. The Bible says in Proverbs 4:11 (NIV), "I instruct you in the way of wisdom and lead you along straight paths." So, according to the Word of God, if we ask, God will help us.

As we end Section 2, I pray the testimonies, both personal and biblically, increase your faith and give you hope to stand on the Word of God. As you meditate on the Word of God, keep 2 Timothy 4:7 (NIV) close to your heart. It says, "I have fought the good fight, I have finished the race, I have kept the faith." I urge you to not give up and run your race.

Section 3

LIVING A LIFE FOR
JESUS CHRIST

As you read this book, I pray it has stirred up a desire within your heart to live a life for God or rekindle the relationship you once had with Him. The first step to living a life for God is to make sure that you're a child of God. The Bible says that all who call upon the name of the Lord shall be saved. Ephesians 2:8–9 (ESV) says, "For by grace you have been saved through faith. And this is not your own doing; it is the gift of God, not a result of works, so that no one may boast." John 3:16 (ESV) says, "For God so loved the world, that He gave His only Son, that whoever believes in Him should not perish but have eternal life." Romans 10:9–10 (NIV) says:

> If you declare with your mouth,
> "Jesus is Lord," and believe in
> your heart that God raised Him
> from the dead, you will be saved.
> For it is with your heart that you
> believe and are justified, and
> it is with your mouth that you
> profess your faith and are saved.

Do You Desire to Live A Life for Jesus Christ?

The exciting part about being in the family of God is that you have a Father who loves and cherishes you. He made you in your mother's womb and He knows every hair on your head. You are the apple of His eye and He loves you so much that He sacrificed His one and only son so your relationship with Him could be restored. Through Jesus's death and resurrection, He provided you with a way back to your rightful place and right-standing alongside our Heavenly Father.

A Commitment to Jesus Christ

If something were to happen to you today, where would you spend eternity? I have had the opportunity to lead many people to Jesus Christ and have heard people respond with, "I go to church," "I am the biggest contributor in the church," "I grew up in the church," "I do a lot of good things for people" and some have flat-out said, "I am going to hell." My response to that would be, let's just fix that right now and clarify where you will spend eternity. So today if you have invited Jesus into your heart then you have assurance of eternity in heaven. If you have never invited Jesus into your heart, pray this prayer, believe it, and receive it.

Dear Heavenly Father, I come to you as a child who wants to make certain of where I will spend eternity. I confess before you that I know that I don't live the best life and could use your help. I confess that I have sin in my life, and I want to make my life right before you today. You said if I confess my sins that you would forgive me. So, right now I say that I am sorry for everything that I have done. Help me to get it right and allow me to have an opportunity to live right before you. I believe that your word is true. You said if I speak with my mouth, "Jesus is Lord," and believe in my heart that God raised Jesus from the dead, that I would be saved. So, God, right now, I take the step in faith to believe that I am saved. You are my God. Jesus is my Savior and the Holy Spirit is here to help me walk as a child of God. Thank you, God, for a second chance. Thank you that I am now a

*child of God and belong to the heavenly
kingdom. I pray in Jesus's name.*

Congratulations! You just made the most important decision of your life. Welcome to the family of God. You are a child of God and now joint-heirs with Jesus Christ. Romans 8:17 (ESV) says, "If children, then heirs—heirs of God, and joint-heirs with Christ…" Ask God for wisdom that He will guide you in all the affairs of your life. Trust in God so He can help turn your life around and provide you with a fresh new start in life. It is important to read the Bible and find a good church that teaches the Word of God. Your pastor will help you grow and mature in the Word of God. Your pastor and the Holy Spirit living deep within you, will teach you how to live your life for God.

If you just accepted Jesus Christ as your personal Lord and Savior, please send me an email and tell me your story. I am so excited for you and would love to hear how God is touching and changing your life. I have also included our website address so you can learn about the many exciting things happening in the ministry, Living in the Light Women's Ministry International, and check out other products available in the online store.

Email: livinginthelightwmi@gmail.com
Website address: livinginthelightwmi.com or connect with Facebook at https://www.facebook.com/ScriptureScript.

Scriptures to Encourage You in Your Walk with Jesus Christ

Now that you have decided to follow Jesus Christ, I want to leave you with some scriptures from the Bible in the Amplified Version. Read these scriptures out loud and declare them over your life. Let the Word of God sink in and transform your thought life. As we close out this book, I want to share one final verse. Philippians 4:8–9 (NIV) says:

> Finally, brothers and sisters,
> whatever is true, whatever is noble,
> whatever is right, whatever is pure,
> whatever is lovely, whatever is
> admirable—if anything is excellent
> or praiseworthy—think about such
> things. Whatever you have learned or
> received or heard from me, or seen
> in me—put it into practice. And
> the God of peace will be with you.

Salvation Scriptures

> "Guide me in Your truth and
> teach me, For You are the God
> of my salvation; For You [and
> only You] I wait [expectantly]
> all the day long" (Ps. 25:5).

"For God alone my soul *waits* in silence; From Him comes my salvation" (Ps. 62:1).

"For God so [greatly] loved and dearly prized the world, that He [even] gave His [One and] only begotten Son, so that whoever believes and trusts in Him [as Savior] shall not perish, but have eternal life" (John 3:16).

"And it shall be that whoever shall call upon the name of the Lord [invoking, adoring, and worshiping the Lord—Christ] shall be saved" (Acts 2:21).

"And there is salvation in no one else; for there is no other name under heaven that has been given among people by which we must be saved [for God has provided the world no alternative for salvation]" (Acts 4:12).

"He then brought them out and asked, 'Sirs, what must I do to be saved?' They replied, 'Believe in the Lord Jesus, and you will be saved—you and your household'" (Acts 16:30–31 NIV).

"I am not ashamed of the gospel, for it is the power of God for salvation [from His wrath and punishment] to everyone who believes [in Christ as Savior], to the Jew first and also to the Greek" (Rom. 1:16).

"For whoever calls on the name of the Lord [in prayer] will be saved" (Rom.10:13).

"Therefore, if anyone is in Christ, the new creation has come: The old has gone, the new is here!" (2 Cor. 5:17 NIV).

"God made Him who had no sin to be sin for us, so that in Him we might become the righteousness of God" (2 Cor. 5:21 NIV).

"For it is by grace you have been saved, through faith—and this is not from yourselves, it is the gift of God—not by works, so that no one can boast" (Eph. 2:8–9 NIV).

"But [we are different, because] our citizenship is in heaven. And from there we eagerly await [the coming of] the Savior, the Lord Jesus Christ" (Phil. 3:20).

"This is good, and pleases God our Savior, who wants all people to be saved and to come to a knowledge of the truth" (1 Tim. 2:3–4 NIV).

"But you are a chosen people, a royal priesthood, a holy nation, God's special possession, that you may declare the praises of Him who called you out of darkness into his wonderful light" (1 Peter 2:9 NIV).

"Behold, I stand at the door [of the church] and *continually* knock. If anyone hears My voice and opens the door, I will come in and eat with him (restore him), and he with Me" (Rev. 3:20).

If you declare with your mouth, "Jesus is Lord," and believe in your heart that God raised Him from the dead, you will be saved. For it is with your heart that you believe and are justified, and it is with your mouth that you profess your faith and are saved.
                    Romans 10:9–10 (NIV)

My dear children, I write this to you so that you will not sin. But if anybody does sin, we have an advocate with the Father—Jesus Christ, the Righteous One. He is the atoning sacrifice for our sins, and not only for ours but also for the sins of the whole world.

1 John 2:1–2 (NIV)

BIBLIOGRAPHY (REFERENCES)

Berry, Linda. Personal Testimony. 2020. Permission for printing.

Bible Hub. (2004-2020). Retrieved from Biblehub.com: https://bible.com. Berean Study Bible.

Bible Hub. (2004-2020). Retrieved from Biblehub.com: https://bible.com. Contemporary English Version.

Bible Hub. (2004-2020). Retrieved from Biblehub.com: https://bible.com. English Revised Version (ERV).

Bible Hub. (2004-2020). Retrieved from Biblehub.com: https://bible.com. English Standard Version (ESV).

Bible Hub. (2004-2020). Retrieved from Biblehub.com: https://bible.com. International Standard Version (ISV).

Bible Hub. (2004-2020). Retrieved from Biblehub.com: https://bible.com. King James Version (KJV).

Bible Hub. (2004-2020). Retrieved from Biblehub.com: https://bible.com. Good News Translation.

Bible Hub. (2004-2020). Retrieved from Biblehub.com: https://bible.com. New American Standard Bible (NASB).

Bible Hub. (2004-2020). Retrieved from Biblehub.com: https://bible.com. New Heart English Bible.

Bible Hub. (2004-2020). Retrieved from Biblehub.com: https://bible.com. New International Version (NIV).

Bible Hub. (2004-2020). Retrieved from Biblehub.com: https://bible.com. New Living Translation Version (NLT).

Bible Hub. (2004-2020). Retrieved from Biblehub. com: https://bible.com. New King James Version (NKJV).

Huebschman, Eric and Bekah. Personal Testimony. 2020. Permission for printing.

Kalicharan, Sean, and Natacha. Personal Testimony. 2020. Permission for printing.

Peterson, E.H. (2018). Bible Gateway. Retrieved from https://www.biblegateway.com. The Message (MSG). Obtained 10-2-2020

Quote Master. Retrieved 9/24/2020 from Https://www.quotemaster.org/ Picture+Is+Worth+A+Thousand+Words.

Ramirez, Nina. Personal Testimony. 2020. Permission for printing.

The Bible App. (2008-2019). Retrieved from bible.com: https://www.bible.com. Amplified Version (AMP).

OTHER PRODUCTS/RESOURCES

Connie Elliott is founder, president, and CEO of Living in the Light Women's Ministry International, LLC located in Sebastian, Florida. She developed Scripture Script (SSx) which includes nine different products to assist the body of believers to stand firm on the Word of God. The idea was given to her by God in April 2019. The idea was developed, produced, and sold beginning in March of 2020.

Connie is the author of *Be Encouraged*, which was released in October 2020. It is available through Trilogy Christian Publishing, Amazon, Barnes and Noble, Books a Million and available in electronic version.

To learn more about the ministry, request a speaking opportunity, or purchase one of the SSx product lines, visit the online store at livinginthelightwmi.com or you may contact by email at livinginthelightwmi@gmail.com.

ABOUT THE AUTHOR

Connie Elliott and her husband, Leslie, live in Sebastian, Florida, and have been married for thirty-four years at the time of this printing. They have five grown children and four grandchildren. They have spent their years investing in their family, setting an example of God's unfailing love, and helping their children to stay strong in their faith and walk in God. Walking a life for God may not always be easy based on the choices and decisions one has made for their life but God's word says He will always be with us. We are never alone.

God's word says that He gives us the desires of our hearts. Connie has desired to write books for God and encourage people to press into the call of God that has been placed on their lives. She desires that when this book is read, it will give you hope, faith, and encouragement in the possibilities of God, knowing in your heart that with God, all things are possible. Just as the Holy Spirit gave the Apostles in the New Testament the ability to write letters. It is also Connie's desire to write encouraging words that will give inspiration to all who read her books.

It is Connie's prayer that you continue growing in God's word and share with others the goodness of God in your life. We must remember to never give up on God. The one scripture that Connie continually stands on in her life is Galatians 6:9 (ESV). It says, "And let us not grow weary of doing good, for in due season we will reap, if we do not give up." Don't give up! You may want to but don't. In your weakest moments, speak the word. Speak what you want, not what you have. You will be amazed at how God will turn situations around as you continually look to Him and place your trust in His goodness and unfailing love.